Against Translation

ALAN SHAPIRO

Against Translation

THE UNIVERSITY OF CHICAGO PRESS

Chicago & London

The University of Chicago Press, Chicago 60637
The University of Chicago Press, Ltd., London
© 2019 by The University of Chicago
Published 2019
Printed in the United States of America

28 27 26 25 24 23 22 21 20 19   1 2 3 4 5

ISBN-13: 978-0-226-61350-5 (paper)
ISBN-13: 978-0-226-61364-2 (e-book)
DOI: https://doi.org/10.7208/chicago/9780226613642.001.0001

Library of Congress Cataloging-in-Publication Data

Names: Shapiro, Alan, 1952– author.
Title: Against translation / Alan Shapiro.
Description: Chicago ; London : The University of Chicago Press, 2019. |
    Series: Phoenix Poets | Includes bibliographical references.
Identifiers: LCCN 2018031840 | ISBN 9780226613505 (pbk. : alk. paper) |
    ISBN 9780226613642 (ebook)
Subjects: | LCGFT: Poetry. | Autobiographical poetry. | Prose poems.
Classification: LCC PS3569.H338 A73 2019 | DDC 811/.54 [B]—dc23
LC record available at https://lccn.loc.gov/2018031840

♾ This paper meets the requirements of ANSI/NISO Z39.48-1992
(Permanence of Paper).

CONTENTS

ACKNOWLEDGMENTS

I wish to thank the following journals and magazines in which these poems or versions of them first appeared:

Baffler: "Justice"
Cherry Tree: "Gary"
Greensboro Review: "Patience"
Plume: "Family," "First Love," "Wheelies," "Hurricanes," "Father," "Geese," "Hands," "Puberty"
Poetry: "Against Translation"
River: "Buddy," "Late Desire," "Letter to Kathy"
Threepenny Review: "Encore"
TriQuarterly: "Devotion," "Outcast" (formerly titled "Afterlife"), "Smell," "Manhood," "Hell"

Also, thanks to *Poetry Daily* for featuring "Encore."

"Against Translation" was translated into French and published at the online poetry magazine Catastrophes (http://revuecatastrophes. wordpress.com).

One

AGAINST TRANSLATION

The songs swept down from the northern steppes
with cinerary horse
and sword and vestment
in the wake of battle
suicidal for a bronze
translation of flesh burnt
to a vertical vapor trail
of fame that, so they claimed,
would be undying,
by which they meant
the dying would be just
prolonged
a little longer
as on a ladder
made of air each
legendary smoke of name could only climb
by thinning
till it wasn't there.

And now as the steel tips of our devices
dig, sort through
and analyze
what's left behind,
scant traces
of berserk debris, dumb soot of ritual effaced
by dumber ash,

3

beneath ghost towns
the ghosts have all abandoned,
all we unearth
intact now
are the untranslated
bones of babies,
inhumed at home in older dwellings
on deeper strata
under mud floors
in pits—placed
carefully on sides, knees drawn to chests,

skulls cupped in pebble bones of hand,
the dead nursling,
the stillborn,
the miscarried—unnamed,
unadorned,
as if the only grave goods
buried with them were
their perishing,
as if that
were what the mothers
wanted to keep close,
keep hidden, safe
from the heroic
stench of burning
upward while their breasts
still swelling, dripping
freshened the black dirt
sucking at their feet.

MANHOOD

You were still too little for the new bicycle I'd gotten you but too big for the tricycle you still liked to ride, and so while the big bike stood unused in the driveway, you rode the tricycle around the cul-de-sac, knees banging on the handlebars, feet clumsily pedaling, happy to be too big for once for anything, laughing so goofily it made me laugh to see you laugh, which as I watched surprised me the way the plane-less silence in the skies that week surprised us all. 9/11 had just become itself. A new and heady unironic language you couldn't speak without and still be heard had overnight become our lingua franca, an Esperanto we woke up knowing, as if what tumbled down with the towers were the civic Babels of our separate lives, as if we had been blown by the explosions backward to a pre-Babel, nearly Edenic understanding, speaking the same tongue inside the same body politic that flexed its outraged muscle through the words we spoke, no matter whom we spoke them to. Our good neighbor Rob, the Vietnam vet, business school professor, church deacon, town council member, wandered over to where I stood. You were shouting "watch me daddy watch me," and as you pedaled by he said, "Big boy like you shouldn't ride a girl's bike." The barb of mockery was aimed at me, it seemed, not you. Yet you, not understanding what or why, you got it. Something wasn't right—something I hadn't told you about except perhaps in my too soft, understated, overnuanced way, conveyed without explicitly conveying, reluctantly, in stifled anger and impatience, in signals flashing by too quickly to notice even while they're felt. You looked at him and then at me, and in the look I saw inchoate bafflement, trace elements of shame, first inklings of an aura of the law that through him, at that moment, had finally found you out. And as you pedaled off, you were just like us now, not smiling, not laughing, serious and dutiful: you too had a job to do, so you did it.

PREPOSTEROUS

To picture the infinitely
knotted up and tangled
ganglia of all life
in reverse, receding
like tipped over dominoes
tipping back
up to a first
not yet tipped over
into everything,

or back before that to that
four-billion-year-old
first billionth of a nano-
second of a ghost
speck of no longer now
about to be, of lowest
entropy
that being anything,
by virtue of being, could permit,

to imagine
there inside it
in its next to nothingness all
possible combinations of all
somethings—the past
still in the future

and the future in the just
now not

even dreaming past now to itself—
and then to think how we too
were there, how the sheer
infinitesimal
nano-chance of us
was there already
as the un-
likeliest of crapshoots in that pre-
coalescing
of post-

nothing, makes me
wonder in the aftermath of
yet new carnage
if there isn't
something of that nothing
we began as
even now inside us grown
so tired of the attempt
at waking

into something
that it wants to just
go back
to what it was, to
sleep, to have the
whole thing over with
already, tiredness

so extreme
it hardly feels

the tribal bolt lock
sliding shut,
the finger itchy on the trigger
and the shoulder
against the buttstock
braced
for the automatic
bang and recoil.

CUBAN MISSILE CRISIS

The pipe smoke as smell when Uncle Charlie smoked it, the blue-gray, lazy, undulating bands above his head like a visual expression of the burly sweetness in the nose, and the pipe as taste when I'd sneak a hit, the sickening oily ash now burning on the tongue and in the throat, and how, despite that, the smell and look of it still made me want to try again, as if the bad taste had been all my fault, and next time would be different, though it never was. The film clips of the atom bomb exploding—so beautiful on the outside, the concentric soft flash at the moment of the blast, and the way organically and slowly it would rise out of itself, pulsing up into a still tornado, colossally calm on the TV screen until you saw it from the inside where blizzard gales of ash incinerated houses, whole towns and cities, bodies vaporized to streaks of charcoal on the ground. Or the way aluminum siding turned our gray house in a single day so brightly white you had to think only a family of angels could have lived inside it while inside it on that day we were almost like angels, sitting in quiet all afternoon and evening before the TV as our warships encircled Cuba, halos of smoke from Charlie's pipe spreading out above us all, the fear a kind of closeness, the cramped rooms for once no longer spacious with disaffection. Outside the Soviets were coming; inside, nobody was at anybody's throat.

BYSTANDER

"I saw a man put together what was left of his son in a bag."
—*USA Today*

The words as I read them looked up at me from the screen as if I had blundered in on a private meeting and everyone in the room at once stopped speaking, waiting for the dumb intruder to realize his mistake and leave.

The phrase I-saw-a-man looked up out of the aftermath of what had happened when words again could happen but only as mute marks speaking a Siri kind of sound, a put-together-what-was-left sound, sound of speaking dis-intoned, devocalized, and thus unable of-his-son to make its speaking in-a-bag heard or known.

When someone calls or knocks, we say, "Who is it?" The sexless, voiceless voice of the words was like an it too. More it than who. And the it of the voice was like the it of the bag—in that it wouldn't tell me if the bag was plastic, clear, and ziplocked. Or white, or black, or dark green, cinched like the giant kind we use to haul dead leaves away.

And the collection of *its* that was now all that was left of the son, that the father—machinelike, or like a zombie, or a howling zombie, a weeping, sleepwalking it?—tried to put back together in the bag, to make it less like it was now and more like what it had been when it was he, boy, son, what parts were those and how in the bag exactly were they put together, or does put-together just mean dumped higgledy-piggledy into the bag, jumbled by the bag into a heap?

The day had been like any other day until it wasn't, and before it would be again, the voice repeated what it saw. And maybe it shrugged, then, or wept, or howled, or just shook its head, but whatever it did, there was nothing else for it to do now but walk on to wherever it was going, namelessly and sexlessly, out of the words it spoke through into the empty screen.

HURRICANES

for A. Van Jordan

Long before King or Selma, Du Bois or Baldwin; before I'd heard
of minstrel; before there were words or concepts in my mind like
white flight, Jim Crow, lynch, ghetto, slavery, or riot; before anyone
or anything existed beyond the family and the neighborhood, and
the only black person I knew firsthand was Melba, my mother's sixty-
something-year-old maid, whom my mother referred to as her "girl,"
the only adult in my world I didn't have to call Miss or Mrs., who
came by bus from nowhere to clean the house, then disappeared
by bus until the next time when (I may have thought) we'd bring
her back to life to clean for us; before there was news or history,
even police, there was *Amos 'n' Andy*. Like everyone, I loved the
big-jawed, ever-scheming Kingfish and his shrill wife Sapphire "the
blue moon," and Mama, his shriller mother-in-law. I loved Lightning,
too, the slow-as-molasses Stepin Fetchit knockoff, though back
then I hadn't heard of Stepin Fetchit; and the lawyer whose name,
Algonquin Calhoun, I'd say out loud because it made my parents
laugh to hear me say it, though I never quite knew why because to
me in my voice it expressed a kind of power, status, and exotic dignity
even if Algonquin himself, as I recall, was short and thin and utterly
ineffective. I even asked my parents, if they would, to please call me
Algonquin, not Al—Algonquin Calhoun Shapiro—which of course
they never did, though this too amused them greatly, so I continued
asking. But what I couldn't wait to see each week was Calhoun's spare,
neat office, no book anywhere in sight, and the desktop, massively
stark with just a black phone in one corner, an inkwell with no
pen in the other, and in the middle a giant blotter, so purely white

against the dark wood of the desk that it embodied nothing if not total order and coherence, and thus became for me the calm eye of the hurricane of riotous mishaps, pratfalls, and entanglements that Kingfish whirled across the screen each week. Last week, in a different episode, in a different kind of weather, the police on my television screen, in black riot gear and standing shoulder to shoulder perfectly still in a straight line, faced a crowd restlessly coming and going in the street, a few on bikes, but most on foot: all shouting and shaking fists or now and then hurling something while behind them a CVS is burning, and a car overturned is burning too, and absurdly out of the maelstrom, as if both to hold it off and to answer for it, I'm back inside that eye where all you can hear is the laugh track, while outside in living color the windows implode into a whirlwind of screams and shattered glass as the blotter spirals off, and the inkwell too, and before it vanishes the fake phone, ripped from its cradle, is ringing as it goes round and round so that whoever's on the other end might hear.

JUSTICE

Less for the murders than the smug face
remorseless smirking on the screen
all through the trial, when I heard how
he had greased the floor with shampoo
before he hanged himself so when his legs
thrashed his feet would just keep slipping
to increase the pressure they, despite him,
were frantic to relieve,
                        when I pictured or
tried to picture the cramped abyss of the dark
cell in which his body jerked and kicked,
pissing itself till it finally hung limp, dripping,
it was as if I'd staged the suicide myself
in a godly fantasy of payback, eye for eye, redress,
but the scales just wouldn't stop trembling,
quivering, off-kilter but barely, almost
but never quite still, or even, like an undershirt
I may have blindly put on backwards or inside out
because now it fits and doesn't, isn't right and is.

PHOTOGRAPH OF NEO-NAZI MARCH THROUGH SKOKIE, ILLINOIS, 1977

for Patricia Evans

How just like the shoelace no one ever sees untie itself
the signifiers from the signified
come loose and fray
and drift away, promiscuous,
as if they had no past
while promising to whatever they happen to
alight on undying love and devotion.

The way the handsome teenage boy could be a Woodstock refugee,
if it weren't for the German cross dangling from his ear,
the swastika pinned to his beret,
just look at his goatee's
shadowy scruff, its stylish
unkempt nonchalance, as if it happened accidentally
or naturally
the way his ponytail
cascades so liberally
from the back of his beret,
and from the way
his mouth half open almost smiling, his eyes half closed,
chin slightly raised
is saying something
in a blissed-out undertone
to or about the old Jew
screaming at him from across the barrier,
amused by how "uptight" the old Jew is,

that's maybe how a boy of that time would have put it,
what's maybe on his almost smiling lips.

Uptight, a word coined in the jazz dives
of the nineteen forties and fifties, a compliment back then
meaning at one with,
in synch with, as in that dude is uptight with his instrument.
But the signs loosen, fray, and drift;
the signified forlornly wait for what they'll be.

The boy is all composure, quietness, inner peace.
He's chill, one might say, today,
in coolness, reposing,
as Dr. Johnson says,
in the "stability of truth," a good
looking boy (if you just go by appearances)
unravished and at peace
like the quiet happy lover
on an urn that some of us believed
in its very stillness stood for truth and beauty,

whereas the old Jew with crooked wicks
of white hair sticking out as if electrified,
or tasered (if this were nowadays),
his forehead wrinkled from the shock of screaming,
his mouth stretched wide disfigured by the scream,
neck veins engorged, he's all
unquiet ravishment, uptight with the antithesis
of what the boy is uptight with, each
defining what the other means, or doesn't—
the signified, the hippie Nazi and the hate-warped Jew,

fixed there and looking on forever at each other
as on an urn
the signifiers falling into quietly as ash
will never fill.

Two

ANCESTRY

In the same way the sunglasses I'm wearing in the snapshot, the sunglasses I never failed to wear throughout my later years, could not prevent or slow the macular degeneration that made those later years so awful, so humiliating, so tedious for everyone, my wife especially, that when my death did come they all rejoiced, however guiltily, behind their show of grief, so you yourself should never think this snapshot of the two of us on the beach together more than sixty years ago, of me shirtless in long white pants, black socks, black shoes, holding you a naked toddler in my lap, neither of us smiling, enlarges you by linking you to me, or that it could in any way shorten the distance between here and there, or that these words in a language I never spoke, that you pretend I'm speaking now, might ever look out from behind the shades I'm wearing and see what I was seeing at the moment when the shutter closed.

FATHER

To him, business was all that mattered. And in business you either gave a fucking or took a fucking. Unfortunately, he was almost always the one who took, not the one who gave, whereas according to him I was a chemist when it came to money: if I had it I turned it into shit. The few times he had it he invested in the stock market, and the investments mostly tanked or flatlined, until he sold them, then they rose. Still ever hopeful he'd explain: "You have to speculate to accumulate. The only thing that grows when you hold it is your pecker." Of a man who had no taste in clothes, he'd say his collar didn't match his cuff. Of a man he didn't trust, he'd say, "He'd fuck a snake if he could get down low enough." When I was twelve, and it was time, according to my mother, for me to know about the "birds and bees," he called me into the bedroom while he was cleaning his golf shoes with a knife, digging dried mud out from between the cleats and flicking the bits and pieces onto the newspaper at his feet. Head bent over the upturned shoes, he never looked up or paused in his work. "Al," he said, "you're almost a man now, so keep it covered. Now get lost." When I told him I wanted to be a poet, he asked me if I was queer. One Sunday afternoon, my brother and I were roughhousing with him on the floor of the den, which we often did and loved doing though it was frightening, which was part of the fun, how truly manic he would get, eyes crazed, mouth frothing, speaking some foreign tongue made of grunts and laughter as he threw us up and down against each other, tickling us just hard enough for us to feel what else he could do if he decided to, communicating through the play a violence way beyond the play, and from somewhere else in the house my mother came running, thinking we were screaming in earnest, which we may have been: "Get off them," she cried, "get off them!" and raised her hand as if to strike him and he scrambled up from the floor so quickly she fell back against a wall and now his hand was raised and she was cowering, arms up like a shield in front of her face—quietly he said, "Don't ever," and the menace in the quiet said playtime was over. If he saw a white woman with a black man in public walking arm in arm, he'd say under his breath, "Take him home to meet your mother." Then to us he'd say, "When you walk through a field of clover you smell like clover; when you walk through a field of shit you smell like shit." Yet on her deathbed he begged his own daughter, whom he'd disowned for marrying a black man, to forgive him for his stupid bigotry. What he never thought of didn't exist until he thought of it, which he seldom did. My mother called him the most selfish man she'd ever known. He called her a frigid bitch. If anything was wrong with any of us, he'd be sick with worry, but otherwise he didn't need to see us, often didn't want to see us, and when he did see us he couldn't wait for us to leave. Once he retired and until he went blind, he watched CNBC all day long, following the stock prices passing in the crawl bar at the bottom of the screen. We had almost nothing to say to each other. He was short-tempered, bullheaded, anxious, unreflective, handsome, loyal, charming, utterly miserable in his marriage but otherwise, as he would put it, "A-OK, copacetic, aces."

GROUNDERS

The field he took me to was all dirt and pebbles and small stones, no grass, no diamond, no plate or bases, and for some reason the town oiled the stones and pebbles, which made the field slick as well as bumpy and smell like an old garage. The balls he'd hit at me bounced angrily any which way up over my glove against my chest or face until I couldn't keep my head down or eyes open, bruises all along my arms and chest, my neck. It was like learning something that's the opposite of skill, since the more he made me practice, the worse I got, the less confident, more fearful. In the oil-blackened field the stones and pebbles glimmered under the noon sun like distant planets, each one made of fields I'd have to practice on forever. The difference between night and day or black and white was the difference between his voice and his body, the way his voice, so kind, so patient, kept shouting out encouragement, I could do this, I was a big boy, he was so proud of me, while he swung the bat a little harder each time, and the grounders I never caught skidded at, against, or by me, through my legs or over my shoulder, so we couldn't stop. And the love increased as the errors mounted. Head down, eyes open, who knew how far I'd go? He could see the talent, even if I couldn't. This was the greatest country on earth, and even if he'd worked his whole life like a dog and never had more than a pot to piss in, everything for me was possible. Sad, kind, more than a little angry, like Moses glimpsing through me a promised land he'd never enter, and making sure that if I entered it I'd remember what he'd taught me, or my body would, and if I didn't I'd know who to blame.

SHOELACES

I never saw my shoelaces come untied. It didn't matter who had tied them for me, or, when I was old enough, how carefully I looped the loops myself, then tied and tugged the loops into a knot tight as a pebble; still by increments too miniscule, too subtle to feel or see, they over hours step by step would loosen to disadhere, to disentangle, sliding free in ways no one in the history of shoes has ever yet recorded. It happened only when you looked away. It happened only when you weren't aware. Awareness of it was itself a measure of the very thing you missed, the thing you couldn't perceive directly, only after the fact, or by effects it had on other things. How the foot felt suddenly slipping from the shoe; how tall grass darkening as it bent on a distant hillside for a moment was the wind made visible, "the shadow of the wind," just as the same grass you couldn't see yellowing as it yellowed till it yellowed was the shadow of time. The shadow of a force so patient, so busy everywhere at once I couldn't and still can't "rid the thought" of it "nor hold it close." Even now, the atoms of those laces of those long-ago lost shoes and sneakers—tied up however tightly into other things—are coming loose and slipping free and being blown round in a wind no one can feel looping the spinning planet as it loops the sun.

FAMILY

None of my friends called their grandmother Nana. Only I did. And mine wanted to be called Nana probably for the same reason years before she insisted that her only child, my mother, even as a baby, call her Lee. To be younger than, better looking than, happier, more alive than—that was all that mattered, and it mattered more with every stroke (the first at forty-eight) until by fifty, fat, infirm, and shuffling, she could hardly dress or clean herself, like a child now herself, an incontinent, angry, haughty, indignant child who once a month all through my childhood and adolescence put on a good dress, jewelry, gloves, and with a black pocketbook dangling from her shoulder toddled bravely from the house, breathless and panting, her makeup streaked with sweat, muttering curses at whatever god or force had done this to her body, down to the beauty parlor to get her hair dyed blond and permed and her nails done. If I were by myself and saw her coming, I'd hide or run, hearing her shout after me what she swear-to-god would do when I got home; with friends, I'd pretend not to see her hoping they hadn't, and if they had and laughed at the crazy old fat woman, I'd laugh along as well, as if I didn't know her, even if she called my name. But of course I did know her, and they knew it, though I told myself they didn't, told myself daily that she was separate and other, no concern of mine, no connection. It was a little game I invented, imagining I was nothing but my body, that nothing tied me to what was not me, so I could be the opposite of her, immune to her, entirely distinct and disconnected as my body in its arrogant youth and health was from hers in its sick and misshapen arrogant old age. I played the game of no relation until there was no relation left to be related to, so that in dreams now when I am back there on the street she's baby-stepping down, I don't hide or run but stand there admiring her bravery, wanting to tell her so until I realize I have no voice, no tongue to speak with, no body to move, like a ghost she doesn't see or couldn't be bothered seeing as she toddles up to and through and past me toward the disappearing child she's calling to come back if he knows what's good for him, come back and help his Nana to the beauty parlor.

DEVOTION

Until the next time, this was the worst time. On the way to see her at the nursing home, he told me to pull over, he needed to go bad, god damn it, and hurried into a Best Buy and fifteen minutes later when he hadn't returned I went to find him, and found him in the men's room outside the stall he hadn't made it to in time, pants shackling his ankles soaking wet, and nearby on the floor an embarrassed and disoriented turd. He himself just stood there, face without expression, stoic, looking at nothing, saying nothing, as I cleaned him best I could, the white pants dark and damp through the crotch, which as we left the store he tried to cover with his hands as if he wore no pants, like Adam naked for the first time ever in the Garden when he heard the footsteps of the Lord approaching, which were the footsteps of the shoppers milling everywhere around us in the Best Buy on a weekend of a giant sale. I wanted to take him straight home but he insisted we go on with the visit; she'd be expecting it, his pants were almost dry, what difference did it make at this stage, and if we didn't show I knew as well as he did there'd be hell to pay.

HANDS

There were the aftereffects of surgery. Then there were the aftereffects of the measures taken to undo the aftereffects, and the emergency measures taken to undo what the first measures had done. Two weeks later, I drove her home. Home to her husband who had been so sick with worry he didn't know whether to shit or go blind, and whom now that she was finally going home she dreaded seeing because she didn't have it in her anymore (as if she ever had) to run and do for him, never mind manage his meds, cook, clean, bathe him like a baby and OK I'd be around to help as much as I could, but I had my own family, didn't I, my own headaches. Sixty-three years. Sixty-three years it's been like this. She was eighteen when they got married. Did I know she's never lived by herself, not ever, not for a second? Sixty-three years—chewing the dry, unleavened bread of better and worse, which no one told them would mean bad and awful. Once I had gotten her from the car to the cottage and across the living room of the cottage to the breakfast nook and got her seated; as she sat there, facing him, her hands on the table, her head down, panting, eyes closed like she had nodded off, and he who was in fact blind was looking at her as the blind do, at and not at her, through her to the nothing he could see, and asking softly, was she okay, was everything okay—that's when she began to weep, weep quietly, her shoulders trembling. He put his hands on her hands, and the Parkinson's tremor in his hands made it seem as if his hands too were weeping for the hands they cupped. As I put away the groceries and cleaned the various messes he had made just in the past few hours, they sat like that and talked, their voices barely audible, like parents in a bedroom late at night, keeping their voices down so as not to wake the children. They sat like that, where sixty-three years had brought them, each telling the other how they were, what had hurt them in the days and weeks they weren't together, and what was hurting now.

GEESE

More dream now than memory, though memory is all it is: after an early dinner, I'm dropping them off at their cottage, beside the artificial pond in the retirement community she loves and he hates. Families of geese are crossing in front of us as they get out of the car: he's in a beige windbreaker and floppy safari hat, she's in a washed-out housedress and sweater, holding the Styrofoam box of leftovers in one hand, the other jiggling the key into the lock, while, nearly blind, he waits behind her, hand on her elbow clutching the fabric of the sweater the way a child does to steady or reassure himself, till she opens the door and, entering, gently pulls him in behind her. Just that and nothing else, the end of another unremarkable, dutiful evening of getting them out, of eating out for a change, eating something other than what he calls that slop you wouldn't feed a dog, so they could sit in a restaurant saying nothing, heads bent rabbinically over plates, as if in study of the fork, machinelike, going slowly up and slowly down. I watch the door close on another outing, another week of filial acquittal, eager to resume my life but for some reason this time I don't immediately drive away. I'm staring at the door that's closed behind them, as if it were the border of the known world on an ancient map beyond which someone has scrawled "Here be Monsters!"—I picture him still in windbreaker and safari hat clinging to the fabric at her elbow as she leads him shuffling into chaos howling across a vast savannah inside the cottage while out here in the falling night geese cluster in the road in front of me, defiant, unyielding, even as I pull out edging forward, honking the horn, leaning on it hard now, yet all they do, without dispersing, is squawk and shit and waddle every which way.

GLAMOUR

For her, it would be wearing an evening gown, big-hooped gold earrings, and a pearl necklace, at a wedding in the ballroom of a country club she couldn't afford. As she glides in on the arm of the husband she has long since stopped imagining he'd be, she's being looked at by everyone, the women especially, and she knows when they see her exactly what is going through their minds. She's like a mind reader in the fantasy, inside herself and outside, everywhere at once, looking out from behind the almost blinding aura of the stunning gown and sparkling jewels and at the same time able to watch herself be looked at and envied. And it adds to the glamour, knowing they will never know the woman she imagines they imagine, not even in their fantasies; to them she's all a dazzling opacity while to her they're all an open book, so utterly transparent that she can picture them as if they're her, and not just there at the imagined wedding, but later when the wedding's over, back in the subdivision, in the humdrum bedroom, in the too-familiar bed, being pawed at in the same old oafish ways, while late at night in a café in Avignon she and the man he's never been are looking out across the glittering harbor, if Avignon even has a harbor.

ENCORE

Cold, that's how I was. I couldn't shake it off, especially
those last days and nights doing all the right things
in the wrong spirit, in the antithesis of spirit, more
machine of son than son, mechanical, efficient, wiping
and cleaning and so having to see and touch what it would have
sickened me to touch and look at if I hadn't left my body
to the automatic pilot of its own devices so I could do
what needed doing inside the deprivation chamber of this final
chapter, which the TV looked out on glumly through game
show, soap, old sappy black-and-white unmastered films.

I was cold all the time, I couldn't shake it off till
I was free of her, however briefly, in the parking lot
or at home for a quick drink or toke, anything
to draw some vestige of fellow feeling out of hiding—
hiding deerlike in a clearing at the end of hunting season,
starved but fearful, warily sniffing the scentless air,
breathing in the fresh absence of her scent too new
too sudden not to be another trap—you're dutiful,
she'd say when I'd come back, as always, I'll give you that.

And I *was* cold: I couldn't help feeling there was something
scripted and too rehearsed even about her dying,
laid on too thickly, like a role that every book-club
romance, soap, musical, and greeting card had been
a training for, role of a lifetime, role "to die for"

and O how she would have played it to the hilt
if not for the cold I couldn't shake—which must have so
enraged her—not my lack of feeling but my flat refusal
to pretend to feel, to play along (was that too much to ask?)
and throw myself into the part so we could both, this once
at least, rise to the occasion of what we never shared.

That final day, for instance, the way the Fighting Sullivans on TV
seemed to watch us watch them as a taunt or dare parade their
small town big war grieving fanfare across the screen,
the five sons killed in battle, only the old man holding back,
not crying when he's told the news, not breaking down or
even touching the wife he still calls mother, a stoicism fraught
with all the feeling he stuffs back down inside him as he grabs
his lunch pail, heads to work, just as he would on any other day,
the only hint of sorrow the salute he gives as the train chugs past
the water tower on the top of which the apparitions of his boys
stand waving calling out goodbye pop, see you round pop—

and as the credits roll she's asking if there's anything, anything
at all about the past, the family, her childhood that I'd like to
hear about before she dies, her voice decked out so gaudily
in matriarchal sweetness that I freeze, I shake my head, say,
no, ma, no, I'm good. And just like that the scene is over,
the sweetness vanishes into the air, into thin air, like the
baseless fabric of the mawkish film, an insubstantial pageant
faded as she nods and grimaces and turns away
relieved (it almost seemed) that that was that. Was us. Was me.
The role that I was born for, and she was done with now.

And yet it's never done, is it. The pageant's never faded.
Shake off the cold and it gets colder. There's just no end
to how cold the cold can get, not even on the coldest nights,
not even if I throw the windows open wide and turn
the ceiling fan on high and lie in bed, uncovered,
naked, shivering inward back into myself as if to draw
the cold in with me deeper, down to the icy center stage
where I will always find her frozen in the act of turning from me
while I stand freezing saying, no, I'm good.

Three

ORACLES

Black boom box of the town loner, one hand propping it on his shoulder, pressing it against his ear, as it blasted a force field of electric outrage all around him as he walked the streets, in his own parade of being no one anybody knew, in black boots, black pants and shirt, neck shackled with austere chains, while a heavy key chain clanged from his belt. Mute but for the blasted sound, the indecipherable screeching, he passed by too quickly to be hassled, to care if he was jeered at or merely seen and then forgotten, just part of the scenery, part of the background, the background's angry edge of caring not at all about him, appearing in our lives the way a stranger might appear by accident in a photograph taken by a loved one of a loved one—a wandering oracle, but of what? What didn't register? What mattered little then, and less now, or mattered, we were certain, unforgettably until it didn't, remembered if at all as just a black blur in a torn-off corner of an absent photograph he's stepping out of, into where for him we all along had been, and for each other soon would be?

FIRST LOVE

Before he happened the body was to me
like weather in a place where weather changed
so little it never needed to be noticed,
a sleepwalk through long spells of fog
effusing inside out and outside in
until one day the feeling for him in my body
made of my body the isolated site
that seeing him could only happen from.
His presence fell impartially as sunlight,
indifferent, needless, blindingly unaware
that I was brightening alone below it,
like Blake's sunflower, fixed, drawn, leaning up toward
the golden clime whose going left so fresh
a dark around me I was grateful for it.

Grateful because so long as it was dark
the wanting could be imageless and placeless,
not a being with of bodies but an in-
between so dense with wanting to be filled
that wanting to fill it was itself the force
that held me at the edge of having what
the wanting somehow wouldn't let me have.
Was he my otherwise? Or was I his
the day he leaned across the front seat to
unlock the door for me the way he had
for others so we could go somewhere the smiling

promised would be mine alone, or ours,
long hair the sheen of corn silk, hand on mine
that on its own refused to pull away

the more I tried to pull it, pulling me after
even while I withdrew, like the sun caught
between collapsing and exploding, which meant
I wanted to and couldn't while I did,
both drawn in and withdrawn held down
and hovering galaxies away above
the small boy looking up from where the wanting
wouldn't let me enter, or escape.
How I grew up is how a black hole shrinks
by sucking into its event horizon
all of the emptiness around it, which
it squeezes to a dot that keeps contracting,
sucking until the space increasing in
the shrinking speck has grown too vast to cross.

MIRRORS

The amusement park of my childhood was called Paragon. Paragon Park. And in it was a "ride" that wasn't a ride at all but a crooked hall you walked through called the Crooked Hall that was in fact a crooked hall made entirely of funhouse mirrors, not just on either side but floor and ceiling too. I pretended to love it because everyone else did or seemed to. Maybe we all pretended to love it, anxious to show the world how confident we were, how free of vanity, that we could laugh in clinical fluorescence at the monsters we became inside it, on one side the body pulled like agonized taffy to a barely human smear, while on the other it swallowed itself up into a paramecium blur, a fat puddle. Jeered at by our bodies warped and morphing all around us, we didn't laugh, or I didn't, not really. The mirror did the laughing for me. It was like being caught inside a nightmare particle accelerator—in which the images I presented to the world were all exploded down into some grotesque confessional essence, the Higgs boson of a self-contempt I hid even from myself, except in dreams, or in sudden eruptions out of nowhere of disgust that had no aim or object, that, not to feel myself, I would have to train on others, usually the weakest ones I knew. Getting older, at least, changed that. Getting older is a new park; it's still called Paragon, though no one goes there for amusement. Yet stuck inside it we still joke a lot, we say things like all mirrors laugh now when we are in them, but while the mirror on one side is a young self laughing at an old self in the facing mirror laughing back, we ourselves don't laugh; we are where the laughs collide and shatter.

GRASSHOPPER

to the little ant that was me,
intrepid Stevie, pretty
Stevie for whom the future
was a foreign movie
without subtitles,
bad boy of the moment
of the high school
parking lot, the hallways
and classrooms too,
flask peeking out
from shirt pocket,
always a little drunk,
or high, a different girl
or boy clinging to his arm,
envy of girl and boy
alike, by me especially despite
my ant ways, my little
drone ambition, glanced
at and envied not
so much for the beauty
as the beauty's fuck-it-
all serenity, magnetic
pull of couldn't-give-a-shit,
the you-know-I'm-me face, bright shock
of blond hair, body tall

and slender flexed
with having, taking,
giving, body both
a shameless dare
and warning, and warned
and dared was how I
ant-like, drone-like,
navigated, tray in hand,
the hormonal roar and milky
sourness of the lunchroom,
the sticky linoleum hubbub
each step had to be un-
stuck from as I searched
for a seat at any table
but his, but never too
far from his, and always
near enough to feel
the dense chill of his
pleasure sitting there
without book, or backpack,
no tray of food before him,
the tight black jeans
I couldn't see and not
hate myself for how
they flaunted what they
only halfway hid
because he never needed,
as I did, something other
than or in addition to
the body to be worthy

later of some safer
version of what the
body craved, redress
or substitute for what
my body wasn't.

All through the body's
spring and summertime
grasshopper that he was
he sang, he danced, he drank
and kept on drinking
even as the warned-of
winter came for him
so early and one drink
became one drink
too many, a thousand
not enough,
and we said, see, see,
head down, avoiding
mirrors, fearing
the body and calling
it virtue, shoulder
to grindstone, decade
by decade laying up
in store these crumbs,
these words by which
his body, unrepentant,
reckless, and still
pretty is singing
to me still: let's see

how well you
dance now that the cold
you've spent your life
preparing for has come.

PUBERTY

I'm probably the only man alive (if not the only man who ever lived) who can tell you exactly when it happened, the very moment I stumbled across that threshold into what I'd be and who I am. It's on a summer evening, I'm playing stickball in the schoolyard, I'm pitching, hurling strike after strike into the white rectangle chalked on the brick wall of the school. I have complete command of all my pitches, nipping the corners with my sweeping curve, my screwball speeding like a fastball toward the head of the batter who ducks just when it breaks back over the plate, my fastball untouchable, all smoke and sizzle. I'm working on a perfect game. Even the older boys playing basketball and the tough kids playing cards have stopped to watch me. I'm the center of the universe. That's when tenth-grader Becky Acres, who had a reputation, and who'd never noticed me before, in miniskirt and halter-neck top, saunters right into the middle of the game, calling time-out, time-out, standing arms akimbo between me and the batter who's looking on, dumbfounded, bat on shoulder, as she asks me to go with her to Summit Hill to get high (and maybe, could she mean this too, play around a little?). What are you nuts, I say, I'm playing now, I'm in the middle of a game, get lost, get outta here, and she smiles, suit yourself, and while we all stare she wanders off so nonchalantly even I know callow as I am there's nothing nonchalant about it. I finish the game. I'm walking home in the dark, reviewing every strike I threw—across the letters, low at the knees, inside corner, outside corner, change-up, fastball—no one of which was even fouled off, unhittable, but Becky's smile keeps interfering, materializing Cheshire-like in the air before me, between me and the batter I'm trying to focus on but now can barely see. It's like I'm pitching through her, at her, then there is no ball, no batter, only her face, that smile, repeating suit yourself as the figure saunters away somewhere inside me, leaving behind this sudden and unshakeable absence of what I didn't want until it wasn't there.

GARY

Because his mother and brother whom we never met worked
    weekend nights (doing what I never thought to ask),
every Friday and Saturday, all through eighth grade, Gary let us
    make their small flat in the projects
our secret hangout, clubhouse, den of minor iniquities, exotic to us
    suburban refugees for its dank air of
danger and neglect, gray couch and caved-in beanbag chair in living
    room: no family photos anywhere, no pictures
of any kind on walls or shelves, only a dusty stereo on an upside-
    down crate next to a rightside-up crate
full of records we sat before in a prepubescent limbo smoking his
    brother's cigarettes as we listened
to Gary, scrawny and bucktoothed, hold forth about his brother
    and the girls he did it with
and how he did it, sometimes in parks, in cars, at school even and also
    right there where we
were sitting, that very floor, that dingy carpet: Gary our cocky seer
    whose every word we were
too callow not to believe, predicting how soon before we'd do it too
    and with whom and in
what positions, and then he'd put on "Louie Louie" and, as if he
    couldn't hear his own falsetto
(more Tiny Tim than Kingsmen), sing the lyrics that to us seemed
    unintelligible, slurred with sexual
vacancies we couldn't imagine ever filling even while he caressed
    that absent mic, eyes closed,

hips churning in earnest as if the girls in other songs he'd also sing
    along to, the Peggy Sues and Mustang
Sally's, were looking at him from a future through inchoate
    atmospheres of adoration for whatever it was
he and the rest of us couldn't wait to do, that he pretended to be
    doing for us. What were we as we sat there
but a silent chorus baffled in the dark beyond the spotlight of the
    show he staged of who we'd be,
abashed by being baffled, mouthing words we couldn't understand.
    And what were we later, returning
from our separate summers, but a slightly older chorus struck dumb
    by the news that Gary had been thrown
from his brother's motorbike and killed? His death another baffling
    vacancy we rushed to fill
with other news and interests, girls, sex even, new songs, new
    friends, shoving all thought of him aside
into a neural limbo where he's stayed, in an oblivion of
    unremembering, there on that ferryboat
adrift in a dead calm as it crosses over into permanent forgetting.
    It's like I've plucked him out from among the others
who have long since joined him, some whose names I don't recall,
    who'd gathered with us in that shabby flat
to listen to him sing of a future that for him remained a vacancy of
    longing while for the rest became
a longed-for vacancy of past the songs must have, at times, brought
    back as torment to their marriage beds,
sickbeds, deathbeds, so that when the furlough of this poem ends
    and Gary's been remanded to his place
among them and the boat rocks, jarring them all from sleep, they'll
    be the ones who briefly sing;

he'll be the one who listens, baffled, fearful, understanding nothing
    of the ghost tones of mock
desire in their wised-up voices—as if (how could it be?) there
    never was for any one of us
early or late a Peggy Sue or Barbara Ann, and nothing's dedicated
    to the one you love, and no it wouldn't be nice
if we were older, and yes, you gotta go, you gotta go now, right now,
    let's go.

SMELL

The check had long since come, and he had paid it. And the restaurant now was empty but for the two of them and the last remaining waiters eyeing them angrily from the darkened far end of the room, all the other tables cleaned, the chairs upside down on the tables, and the floor mopped, except for the area sticky with spilled wine under their table where they sat in silence, two empty bottles in front of her, her glass empty, only a dried spot of red at the bottom of it, though she still held the stem and tilted it this way and that as if to swirl the phantom drink all around the inside of the glass. "Let's go, let's get out of here," he said, for the umpteenth time, glancing at the waiters. "This isn't fair." She looked up at him. He glanced away. What did she see there in his face? Embarrassment, of course, and of course exasperation—how he hated scenes in public, poor boy, her drink-induced outbursts, whether of affection or rage, it didn't matter, he hated both, he feared both equally. She was almost sorry for him: she knew he wanted out, had wanted out for some time now, but she also knew how weak he was, how much he needed her to call it quits, which is why, despite everything she'd put him through, he played along, pretending that he loved her, trumping her every insult with forgiveness to insure he'd be the one who's left behind, not the one who does the leaving; the done to, not the one who did. His boyish face, so cleverly baffled and long suffering, waiting her out. The coward. No, she wouldn't give him what he wouldn't say. She'd let him go on not saying it and suffering. Which is why, when he said, sighing, "Come on, honey, let's go," she told him, "I'm not leaving till my drink is finished." "But your glass is empty," he said, smiling, as if he'd proven something, which she disproved, not smiling, holding the glass up to her nose and breathing in. "I can still smell it."

INFIDELITY

Even if from time to time I've thought about it, I've frankly never had the energy for cheating. The furtive trysts, the secret scheduling, the lies spawned by the scheduling and trysts, the maintenance of the lies, the lies those lies require, never mind the evidence you have to shower off, or dab away, delete, deny, ridicule; or the playacting— playing hurt to turn the accusation back on the accuser till she's the one ashamed, the one apologizing, the one with the problem—who needs the aggravation? At the same time, when it comes to fidelity, the why of it, I'm never honest. I mean, think of the buzzkill: telling your spouse you'd never cheat on them because you couldn't be bothered. Not terribly flattering. Better to cheat on them than tell the truth about why you don't. What I always say is honey I'd never do anything like that to you. I say we owe each other that respect, that dignity. I say I'd never humiliate you, I never have. I never will. I flaunt my faithfulness. I've built a fortress on the high ground of it. Up there, I'm invincible; I can look out in all directions. There are no enemy maneuvers I can't see coming. No surprise attacks. From the safety of my position, I can dream of doing anything I want.

AFTER FLOSSING

The way a wet strand sticks to the finger
when you're finished, sticks more tenaciously
the flimsier it is, and won't be shaken off
or flicked, and even to the free finger
flicking at it clings and clings, so
in her sincere acknowledgment of what
was all just her shit all along, not mine,
and would have driven us apart anyway
no matter what I did or who I was, I can still hear
adhering to and tangled up with it the "but still"
of what I was and what I did—my shit,
in other words—that made her leaving me
leaving her the way we did not only overdue but
easier than it otherwise ever should have been.

MEMORY

Out of an otherwise forgotten day
in the always accidental storm
of electrochemical
forgetting

this one instant for no reason
I can know gets caught
without my knowing
in a neural thicket

where it stays a spoor of nothing-
yet-remembered good as dead,
as never having been until
another

instant on another day that also
will be otherwise forgotten
wakens it like a struck
match in a dark

room and as it flashes while it flashes
I'm somehow at the same time
looking back and forward
at water dripping

from a faucet, swelling down from metal
bright as metal liquefied
and thickening until
it snaps off

like something solid in the kitchen
of a house I'm storming out of
for the last time
not knowing

that it is, or that the last words
and the why and how of who
did what to whom
would vanish

just as surely as our voices did
inside those rooms, all of it
gone entirely beyond
recall except

the constant ticking of the water drops
I didn't notice I was even
noticing until the storm
today blew over

and there it was again more than
a decade later, that sound
on that moment's
outer edges

I didn't know till now was
waiting for this moment
ticking outside in from
all the trees

around another house I also
once believed I'd never
leave, from leaf to
leaf but slowly

as if to keep from falling,
like dormant specks
of lightning
dark still

at the leaf tips where it
beads and thickens,
stretching, ready
to strike.

NEO-PLATONIC

The lover's eye is sunlike,
raylike. With its own light
it illuminates
what it yearns for.
To see is to fire
an unseen
heart-seeking
dart into the eye
of the beloved,
to fire and be fired on,
to pierce and be pierced
in a silent two-way
microfield of
ecstatic shock and awe.

That is, if there is mutual desire
or a charitable heart.

"The dart of an Old man's seeing,
on the other hand, bewitched
by a young girl, because
his eye is cold and slow,
his humor clumsy, will always
fall short of the heart
it aims for
while the sight of her

invades
his every chamber
like an oracular infection."

Which must be why
outside the credit union
yesterday when the girl
slipped past me
quickening her step
without acknowledging
the door I held for her,
just as the door slid shut
behind her, I
                    could see
on the black surface
of tinted glass
my own eyes
behind a smear of glasses
small and dim and
looking back
almost amused
at eyes they hardly recognized
                              before they too
turned
indifferently away.

LATE DESIRE

It is to walk in sand. Or rather
it is—as you walk in sand—to have
to lean forward head down
as if up a steep hill going nowhere,
pushing back against what
gives way growing hotter
against what burns more
pushing back. It is to step toward
another toward and toward still
another endless as the white
crest of each great wave curling
over about to topple inside
of which, if you looked up
before it did, you might see
dazzling confections all along
the glassy volute of the breaker
swallowed up and pounded
into nothing on a shore that seethes
with scatterings of shells, claws,
imprints of claws, sea wrack and trash
strewn about so haphazardly
they never seem to move at all,
like those who trudge your way,
head down like yours and hazed
with spray, unstill intent but never

closer, never farther even while
they shrink inside the sound of breakers
they cry out inaudibly against.

COUNTDOWN

In our last days I'd wake to find you holding up your cell phone,
face half aglow, expressionless through game after game of solitaire
because you said it helped you sleep, relaxed you, the far-off
clicking lull of king sliding under ace, queen under king,
the jack ten nine eight columns growing like a countdown
in the nightly, often night-long, confetti clicking-drift toward sleep
I couldn't help but hear as accusation because I could
sleep, because I couldn't or didn't find a way to release you
from restlessness, or from me, or our day-to-day
sleepwalk through a life I had to leave behind to wake from
only to find, tonight, waking alone in a new house, new bed—I'm now
remembering what I pretended not to notice then, how
when the phone shut off your foot would brush mine lightly
for a moment, sliding up and down the inside of the arch as if to feel
for something, expecting something, before it slid off and you
rolled away.

LETTER TO THE CEMETERY OWNER

Even driving past at seventy I thought
you'd want to know I saw the sign
nailed to the front gate, the large black
"Take Heed" Gothic, vaguely Germanic script
proclaiming Limited Time: BOGO Free.
I saw it and I laughed—limited time? No shit!—
then wondered if laughing's what you had in mind.
I mean, if you really wanted to be funny
wouldn't you have tried a little harder,
offered something more than a bare-bones
(ha ha) reduction of mind's ancestral
soul-quaking terror of the abyss's
total and unending isolation—to BOGO. BOGO?

Couldn't you have flattered us a little,
dressed up in classier garb your crass
obsession with the bottom line—as if
two graves for the price of one might make
being dead a deal to die for?
Where will it end? What's next? A Drive
Thru Viewing for the busy mourner—
pulling up as at a Burger King
or bank beside a giant window where
the coffin raised on stilts is tilted toward you
so you don't even have to stop completely—
why you could pitch it as a drive-by funeral

and here's your motto: Remains to Be Seen,
If So Inclined. My friend, don't get me wrong.
It's not that I'm not interested. I am. I am.
It's just that, well, there's no one in my life
right now to share the extra hole with.
And frankly at my age the odds aren't good.
You could say I'm in the demographic
of the funereally unattached. And as such
what I could use is a grave-site hotline,
make that a tepid- or a cool-line better yet,
a senior Tinder service—call it Cinder, Smolder,
guaranteed to get the soon departed laid
together in a double bed on that first
(and only) blindest of all blind dates.

Because the fact is, pal, I didn't realize
how very interested I am until I passed
your sign and laughing turned by habit
half expecting her, my recent ex, to be
beside me laughing too because
she would have busted a gut, that much I know,
and I miss that, I miss how even at the worst of times
her laugh could for the moment of the laugh
at least dispel the stickiest of disaffections;
it would have been a gift to hear it,
a gift I might have half believed you meant
for me alone, given freely as I drove past
and just as freely, once past, taken back.

Four

TURKEY VULTURE

I stopped running when I saw it
up ahead in the middle of the path,
wrapped in a black shawl of wings,

damaged in some way I couldn't see,
because even as I stepped closer
and could feel, or my body could,

the space between us harden with
hidden signals, warnings, compacts
echoing back through every cell

to the beginning of bodies, still
it didn't move, it just stood there
even as I came near enough

to need to come a little nearer
to the snug, efficient down-hook
of the beak, the reptilian wattle

redly quivering while its red face
kept twitching side to side
so each eye could hold inside

its blackest shining what now
stood over it. That's when
I noticed how the head was softly

wrinkled like a wizened baby's
cauled with black stubble, and how
the wings that far away seemed merely

black were crosshatched with lighter
and darker shades of black inside
of which paler flecks and hues

were flashing—splayed out and
brightening as they began to rise—
whatever I was just then inside

its twitching eye shrank before
the black-robed priestly swelling
up and out of wings inflated now

to twice, three times their size, into
the very gesture of an invocation
of a power my body of itself

without me heeded and backed away
from so the wings could shrivel
back into the dying thing it was.

KINDNESS

The right side of the tern was paralyzed, whether from a broken leg or wing we couldn't tell. When one of us came up behind it so as to lift it from the sand, it tried to scoot away, left wing extended, feathers splayed, flapping against the sand while the left claw scratched and dug pathetically to drag the right claw after it, the body going nowhere, turning clumsily in place like a bedraggled merry-go-round. It was early evening and the tide was rising, breakers collapsing into ragged sheets of foam that each time slid a little closer to us before withdrawing back into the next one coming on. It was almost dark, the beach deserted, except for us on a family vacation, possibly our last one all together. I could, I suppose, go anywhere from here. I could tell you who had been sick for a long time and who would be sick soon. I could flash forward to a hospice vigil, or back to some happier, less troubled time when such a vigil would be inconceivable. Or I could describe how we stood there in a circle around the tern, talking in soft voices about what we should or shouldn't do, whom we should call, how we could protect it in the meantime until help arrived. I could tell you how the air got colder as we talked and that in the cold we each in our own way, to ourselves if not to one another, realized that there was really nothing we could do to save it, and maybe we should just let nature take its course. And wouldn't it be deeply meaningful, pleasing as well as sad, like a Wordsworthian spot of time, like the kind of thing that ought to happen in a poem, if I told you how the tern with one wing flapping whirled round and round until it found itself facing the tide still inching closer, the salt spray beading on its one dead wing, and how just then one of us lifted it up and carried it to dry sand and gently set it down with its back to the ocean so it couldn't see what soon would overtake it? Except, of course, nobody picked it up. It had gotten so chilly, and all of us by then were ready for a cocktail on our last night together. One of us ran ahead up the dark beach to turn the lights on in the summer rental and fix the drinks with which we'd toast again the luck that got us through another year.

LETTER TO KATHY

I'm on my second round
from the deck of a bar
in Provincetown

at happy hour pretending
to write to you even
though I don't know

what to write or why
I'm wondering
if you were here

right now whether you
would find, as I do,
some unfathomable

meaning in the accidental
beauty in the way the
daylight as it falls effuses

across the bay, thickens
and seeps where big and little
sloops and dinghies

rock in place
along the wharf, their
rigging, tangled spars,

and masts swaying
every which way
in the rickety midst

of which the sun flickers
like a match struck
in a wind that won't quite

let it catch or die.
I'd like to think there's
I don't know what, Kath,

a happy accident, a joyful
hour—whose solace is the
pointlessness of seeing

how the same sun
that's like a struck match
over there is right here

now glinting like a
speck of starlight
in the gold stud that

otherwise would be too
inconspicuous to notice
in the nose of the woman

on the barstool next
to me who's staring out
so dreamily, given over

to seeing what she sees
she doesn't hear
her phone facedown

beside her gimlet pinging
and pinging, or maybe
does hear but still

won't turn it over to see
who won't stop trying
to get her to please

pick up and read the news
that could be like
what my phone pinged with

just before I started
writing this to you.
I'd like to think you too

would want to know what so
engrosses her out there
toward the breakwater,

which looks from here
as if it's made of steam,
not stone, low wall

of rip-rap steam across
the blue-green water, steam
from a just-extinguished

fire frozen in the first
still burning instant
of it not yet knowing

it's no longer fire—
so white hot
with not knowing

it will cool and thin
away to nothing that
it never does—even

while it seems to
die into this darkening
over land and water

out beyond both
land and water as a
darker water touching

darker land. Kath,
what I'm trying to say
won't say—or can't—

whatever it is
I should be saying.
And the not said

is abashed because now
the fire that had turned
to steam is turning back

to stone. And the phone
I didn't hear stop pinging
isn't pinging anymore

or even here now,
gone with the gimlet
and the woman too,

though in the letter
I pretend to write you
she's out on the beach,

sandals in hand,
half in bar light, half
in dark water pushing

its fringe of foam so icily
around her feet
she has to lift up

this foot first,
then that foot, over
and over in a little un-

easy dance, a
capering in place in water
she can't stand

still in, or stand to leave.

OUTCAST

I saw her in the shadows of the pub, peeking out from behind a column, watching us, the friends she'd left a moment earlier, "to freshen up" she might have said, or was it to go outside for a smoke, or maybe to say hi to someone who'd just entered, someone the rest of us didn't know? Whatever the excuse, all she did was move off by herself so she could watch us, watch how we all behaved, her good friends, in her absence. Her face half lost in shadow, almost apparitional, fixed on us sadly, or so I imagine now so many decades later, everyone but me there at that table long since in the grave, she herself the first of us to die. Had she been sick already? And if so was the urge to see us there without her a premonition of the cancer, the first sign of its onset? Sadly, wistfully, the way a ghost might, visiting an old haunt, she measured the limits of our love for her by our delight in one another, the laughter and good cheer that went on undiminished in her absence, or, worse, perhaps, seemed to her then more robust and intimate once she was gone. From somewhere beyond the farthest galaxy across the bar, forlorn and destitute as Hawthorne's Wakefield, "outcast of the universe," she studied her life without her in it until like Wakefield she had had enough, returned, sat down, and as if nothing at all had happened, as if she'd never left, fell back into the conversation.

AMBITION

I couldn't tell dawn from dusk. By three in the afternoon, the damp, gray, crooked little lanes and alleyways filled up with coal smoke, which made the shop fronts and the flats appear to drift in the sooty haze, as if at sea. Wherever the haze thinned or creased, a pub light flickered through it like a beacon; where it thickened, a pub light blurred and dimmed. And dawn was a shallower night: it didn't rise, it seeped, it effused itself and not out of the east so much as out of some vague general nowhere of the same non-light of afternoon that now increased in quantity without at all brightening. Drained of color, like an underworld, the place was all shade and moody pallor, as if even the living of it was itself a distant memory, something you couldn't quite call back even while it happened. Or is this only how it happens now, how I need it to happen: the time of day no time at all, the streets damp, empty, deserted, and she whom I betrayed refusing now to step forth from the shadows when I call, turning invisibly away, the city silent with her condemnation? And the glorious dream that made me leave her there, deaf to her cries, shamefaced, blind with ambition, skulking through the haze into the future, where has it led me if not right back into that dirty light where I am, where I've always been, hearing nothing, seeing nothing, taking what I need when I need it while I tell myself I'm not a monster, I'll make amends someday, and if I don't—what difference does it really make, twenty years from now, fifty, a hundred, who's going to remember any of it ever happened?

HELL

Dublin, 1974

The car bomb had exploded not far from Trinity only a few days earlier, and the city was still largely on lockdown. Even the churches near the bomb sites were mostly empty. Only the young like me who didn't know any better and the professional drinkers would venture out to huddle close together at the usual hour in the sour-smelling, dim-lit, smoky dens and parlors of the pub around the corner from my flat. A smoldering turf fire added to the cigarette haze around us and above us making us all seem apparitional to each other as we talked in low voices about what had happened and why and when the next attack would be. Nobody yet had claimed responsibility. Some believed the Provisionals were behind the bombings, killing their own to show us that the troubles up North were here now, now there'd be no escaping them, not anymore; others thought it was the doing of the "fooking" Brits and Ulster Volunteers masquerading as Provisionals to show the world just how barbaric the IRA could be, how you can't negotiate with bloody murderers. What was I doing there, the naïve Yank, an Irish wannabe, living an ex-pat's life far from the middle-class Jewish suburbs he despised. There was a priest who drank with us, I don't remember his name, let's call him Father Frank, who found me amusing in my new, white Aran sweater, my curly long blond hair, my infatuation with all things Irish, its pub life, poetry, and song. He liked to mock me in a good-natured sort of way about my speech habits, tics he called them, so bloody American, how I peppered my sentences with you knows and rights and I means. He liked to tease me gently about my insouciant lack of faith, my Jewish heritage, and how it is we Jews can stand to live without an afterlife, no heaven or hell, no living on except in the fallible and transient memory of others. If you're not there to know you are remembered, what bloody good is it? Better that, I'd shoot back, laughing, than, I mean, you know, burning for all eternity in fire and brimstone, or plucking a stupid harp. We'd banter like that each night till he'd finally say, "Drink up, lad, we can settle this tomorrow." But this night he stared into his shot glass saying nothing, the sleeve of his black suit dusted with ash from the cigarette he absentmindedly was either lifting to his lips or lowering to the ashtray without ever putting down. "Well, Father," someone said, "sure there's a place in hell for murderers such as them." "I believe in hell," Father Frank said to no one in particular, adding softly, almost to himself, "But tell me now, lads, who did Christ die for, if not for them, sure, especially for them?" He took a sip of whiskey. "So then what's hell for?" I asked. And he replied, "Why, to show God's love and mercy." "But how can that be, Father?" I prodded, happy to be bantering again the way we would on any normal night. "How does hell show God's love and mercy?" "Because," he said, looking up and smiling now at everyone, "there's no one in it." And everyone, including Father Frank, roared with laughter, and I laughed too, not knowing why, and blushed, as if the joke had been on me, as if I were what was funny.

BUDDY

As from a spaceship hurtling away beyond the galaxies as he drove home from his local bar (when he could still drive), his voice inside the hissing of the background radiation barely audible going on and on about how lucky "we" were, how easily it could have gone another way if not for the goal-line stand, the penalties, the blown assignments, sacks and circus catches, of a team he only cared about because he knew I did, whose victories became at least for him our brotherhood, made us in his mind a triumphant "we"; not once week after week right up until the Super Bowl and our historic comeback did he ever speak about the treatments, the humiliations of a failing body, or his having to move back in with Florence who by then was living with the man she threw him out for. I wondered, of course, who wouldn't, about the debt he must have felt to his betrayers, his bitter gratitude, if that's what it was, for all their ministrations. But I let him set the terms; I let him have the conversation he desired. Given his situation, that was the least I could do even while I came to dread the drunken voice that floated free in black space untethered to anything but its own sound while I uh-huh-ed to what was too sad and tedious either to hang up on or listen to.

Super Bowl Sunday was the last time I heard from him. I had turned the TV off when we fell twenty-five points behind early in the third quarter. Knowing he would call (no doubt as soon as time expired) and too distraught myself, too pissed off to commiserate, I muted my cell and went to bed. Next morning when I discovered I had missed the single greatest comeback in Super Bowl history, embarrassed by my front-runner's fair-weather lack of faith or passion, I couldn't bring myself to listen to his message, to what I knew would be an endless and ecstatic recitation dogged by other more likely outcomes he had to speak about to prove they hadn't happened, as if the game were still in doubt, might turn out differently if not for the fellowship of telling me about it, as if only telling me about it made it real. Only when he died a few months later did I play the message back. There was no "We did it, Al, we did it!" There was nothing at all—no voice at the other end, no we, no us—only an expectant hiss of background radiation, waiting for me to answer, refusing to hang up until I did.

WHEELIES

No one had died yet. No one had even gotten sick. And those who
were sick or had died were, like the old, only what I had always
known them as and thus became the fixed backdrop of the not me,
the never to be me, the so long as they were that then I'd be this

me doing wheelies over playground blacktop, leaning backward
as the front wheel rose and hung there spinning as I pedaled forward
till it was I, not gravity, that eased it down, and then in spite of gravity
leaning backward made it rise again and hang again obedient

only to the shifting pressure of my lightest touch.
Under my skin throughout my body there was only this
one muscular awareness every wheelie was the outer edges of.
I had no reason not to love my body. Not to be my body.

I lived forever in the Eden of each wheelie while I rode
in figure eights and never slowed or faltered, under sun
I didn't know was burning like a flaming sword
over the gate of being there and doing that—betrayal

only a foreign word in a foreign movie undubbed
on a giant screen of sickrooms no one I would love
had either entered or been carried from, the playground
still a playground, and the boy a boy, not a phantom

in a poem doing wheelies for the old man he'd become.

KEATS

I saw my late brother David last night across the gym, head bent in conversation with someone I couldn't see very well. As I approached David didn't look up to acknowledge me or break off the conversation or introduce me to his friend. It was as if I wasn't there, as if I were the one now who was supposed to do the haunting. As his companion said something I couldn't catch in a voice I almost recognized, David smiled and looked up in my direction; it was a knowing smile, but what the smile knew it wouldn't tell me. The smile was the withholding of what it seemed to say and thus was how it said, "You can't know anything about it, not even what it is." Then he stepped aside, and there I was, as I had once been, forty years ago. Twenty-three years old, and I was holding a book of Keats's letters, opened to a letter Keats, when he was twenty-three, had written to his brother, and in the letter this was italicized: "Our bodies every seven years are completely fresh-materiald. . . . 'Tis an uneasy thought that in seven years the same hands cannot greet each other again." The book was floating in the hands of whom I was when I still had a brother, and the words meant nothing to me, just dead marks on a page. I could see right through the ghost of me, a chalky shadow of a hand holding the book out for me to read while the hand said, "This hand can't greet that hand." Then the band I hadn't noticed launched into a silent number, and people filled the dance floor, and the boy stepped into my brother and disappeared, both lost now to the man I was there among the silent dancers as that man will be to the old man I'm becoming. A fresh-materiald ghost in waiting suddenly dis-haunted by the ghost I was, a ghost made even more remote and insubstantial by the words of an even deader boy whose voice out of the book I now was holding was speaking such immediate unease he seemed just then more alive than I or my brother ever was, or anyone living.

NONSENSE

I'm driving at night into the city on the lower level of the Mystic River Bridge beneath the upper level that makes the lower level more like a tunnel than a bridge. My white headlights are shining into red taillights while white headlights behind me shine bright as day inside my rearview mirror. Bridge like a tunnel, night bright as day, it's like I'm stuck inside an outtake of the nonsense poem I chanted as a kid, except it isn't one bright day in the middle of the night, and no dead boys get up to fight, to face each other back-to-back and draw their guns and start to hack; it's only me at the wheel, and my brother riding shotgun, my dead brother whom my orders are to bring to my dead sister somewhere in the city before the night is out. We're saying nothing though the left side of David's head is shaved and the sutures are like *X*s on a path scrawled by a child on a treasure map of nowhere. The off-ramp takes us down into the middle of a blacked-out district, and we're parked now in front of a giant picture window picturing a blacker black. Picture a child's magic eight ball magnified to the proportions of a city block, a giant round block black as night that when it's shaken whirls out of the very blackness a prediction too luminous to read but instead of words it's Beth's face shining there with no expression. And when it whirls her face (who shook it?) back into the blackness of itself, my brother's gone. And now on the upper level of the bridge I'm driving back across the Mystic River except that up here all the traffic goes against itself, in a slow-motion inverse game of chicken, where red lights inside the rearview now grow larger as they move away and the white lights shrink into pinpricks as they approach. I could die from fright but luckily I too am deaf, dumb, and blind. I say luckily because how else could I have heard my orders, or described to you exactly what I saw?

TEACHING

I volunteered to be the moon because I got dizzy spinning and the moon didn't spin; and as the moon I was told to walk around Ellen Waitzkin, who as earth was spinning slowly as she slowly walked around Harry Feinzig, who got to be the sun. The rest of the class standing in little clusters here and there throughout the room became the rest of the Milky Way, which turned around us in a wider circle, while Ellen spinning circled Harry and I not spinning circled Ellen. Once everyone was spinning and circling like synchronized swimmers in the great pool of the universe, Miss Kelly—leaning against her desk, a Lucky Strike in one hand continuously moving from ashtray to mouth to ashtray, smoke swirling in loose rings about her head— asked us in a voice weakened by emphysema to imagine that all the other students in all the other classrooms were moving too in wider and wider circles at even faster and faster speeds; she asked us to try and realize that we're always at every moment moving at speeds we can't feel, even when we're still, even when we're sleeping. We never stop. But when we finally did stop, because the bell rang and the year was over, our last day of eighth-grade science at Devotion too now over, she stubbed out her smoke and lit another one and stood there looking at us, examining us, for once not chiding anyone, thinking who knew what, certainly nothing that could matter to me then. Having taught for decades now myself, though, I wonder if she even saw us standing there before her, us as we understood ourselves to be, as Ellen Waitzkin, Harry Feinzig, Alan Shapiro, or if she saw some impersonal, unchanging mark by which all change, all time in the universe is measured, a classroom of Peter Pans who year by year never aged while only she aged, while only she grew older and more infirm. The bell had rung and so we all whirled off thoughtlessly into our different lives. Unlike our other teachers, Miss Kelly never asked us to keep in touch, to let her know how we were doing. I never thought of her again, until today. And now this thought too is over. When the page turns, listen to it rest against the other pages: its stillness is the sound of unimaginable speed.

WORDS

It wasn't that she didn't love him while he was alive. It was just easier to love him once his body wasn't in the way. And not because he wasn't comely and tall, he was nothing if not photogenic, and even at the most difficult and complicated times she loved looking at the many photographs she'd taken of him through the years, now safely and obediently stowed in albums neatly laid out on the coffee table for all to see. It wasn't his body per se, but the carnal fact of it itself, its machinery, its systematic stinks and emanations out of appetites that made him anyone with anyone, not him in his essence with her in hers. She swore she could hear them, feel them all night as he lay beside her, the droning and sparking predetermined pathways to predetermined destinations, from the excited pulse place in the wrist and throat and behind the ear and all throughout the jittery grid of it down to the greedy crotch. But all that was over now, done with. Out of the way. And going through his files, readying for publication the stories and essays left unpublished at his death, it was like meeting him all over again, him as he was to her at the beginning when she had known him only through his books before the body interfered. And it thrilled her to discover just how frequently it was her body he would write about, her body made entirely of words imagined by the words that were his body, only words describing how she lay there in a darkened room that only words illuminated, under covers that only words were lifting like a veil.

PATIENCE

Between the kiddie park the town closed for repairs after recent flooding and the new three-story senior center there's a piss-poor wooded area in the bow of a run-off creek where teenagers go at night to drink and smoke but during the day is always empty. I can walk my dog off leash there and when he shits I never have to clean it up. It's hardly woods at all so much as tall bushes, weeds, and a few dead trees swallowed up in dead or dying vines, some thick as the trunks they've twisted up and strangled, a stranded understory shrinking into itself while the town goes on subdividing all around it in a meiosis of cement, blacktop, concrete, steel, and glass. One time, I got there early before rush hour. Sunlight passing level through a prism of leaves broke into variegated greens I had no name for. The air, it seemed, had come alive with green gradations and degrees, a green kaleidoscope the sun had summoned that quivered with a chilly symbolism I could feel but not decipher. At my feet, across the emerald moss shell of a log disintegrated nearly into dirt, a single ant was clambering into and out of melded bands of darker and lighter green, over tufts of moss, which when I looked closer I could see were woven of paler tufts, and those tufts too of even paler and shorter ones, none of which so much as bent under the ant as it went where it was going, where it would get to, no matter what, as if it were the ant articulation of the green shades moving over it as it moved down the crumbling log into the weeds among the crushed and rusted beer cans, the shreds of cellophane and dog shit. Little hoplite genius of a place of unfathomable patience with all the time to accomplish what its tiny ant heart if it had a heart was beating for.

DIARIES

When I moved to Ireland, I started one, a pretentious leather-bound journal my parents bought me as a going-away present, something a bit too certain of its own importance, between whose covers I could perform my private life for all posterity. For that whole year I reported on the weather, which being Dublin was the same from day to day, sunny spells and rain, rain and sunny spells no matter the time of day or season. I recorded what I wouldn't have forgotten anyway, whether I'd written it down or not. I say nothing about what I now recall so vividly forty years later: the stench of burning coal, the coal haze of early evenings, meaning in the winter three o'clock or four, the apparitional chilly aura of it that you moved through and breathed in and felt as if outside you lived inside phantasms of an earlier century. I recorded the names of pubs I drank in, and bits and pieces of conversations with people whose names I don't recognize, whose voices have all dissolved into a stage Irish Barry Fitzgerald brogue, more Hollywood fantasy of Irish than anything anyone there actually spoke. After that year I stowed the diary away in a box that followed me from Palo Alto to Evanston to Chapel Hill, from one marriage to another; it ended up forgotten on the bottom shelf of a bookcase in the living room of a house I thought I'd be living in forever. But when that marriage ended too and I had to move again and was going through my things deciding what to keep and what to throw away, I came across it, my Irish diary, and it creeped me out to read it, not because I remembered so little of what I wrote about but because I felt as if it wasn't mine at all or wasn't me, like I was snooping around in someone else's life, someone whose handwriting resembled mine but whom otherwise I didn't know, had never met. And then where my writing ended, there was this, in the shaky script of my eight-year-old daughter who without my knowing had found the journal and for one day claimed it as her own and without date or detail, the page blank beneath it, had written just this and nothing else—written and forgotten about completely as the journal had forgotten me—"Dear Diary, in case you haven't noticed, this is my first entry."

NOTES

"Against Translation": The details of inhumed babies are based on Gustaf Sobin's *Luminous Debris* (2000).

"Shoelaces": "The shadow of the wind" is from E. A. Robinson's "The Sheaves" (1922); "I cannot rid the thought, nor hold it close" is from Frederick Goddard Tuckerman's sonnet "An upper chamber in a darkened house" (1860).

"Keats": "Our bodies every seven years ..." is from John Keats's letter to George Keats, September 21, 1819.